An artist's study *of*
**MASTER
SELF-PORTRAITS**
—
2

WORKBOOK PRESS LLC
187 E Warm Springs Rd,
Suite B285, Las Vegas, NV 89119, USA

Website: https://workbookpress.com/
Hotline: 1-888-818-4856
Email: admin@workbookpress.com

Ordering Information:
Quantity sales. Special discounts are available on quantity purchases by corporations, associations, and others.
For details, contact the publisher at the address above.

ISBN-13: 978-1-953839-16-9 (Paperback Version)
        978-1-953839-17-6 (Digital Version)

REV. DATE: 09/14/2022

An artist's study of
MASTER SELF-PORTRAITS

VOLUME 2

THOMAS CRAWFORD

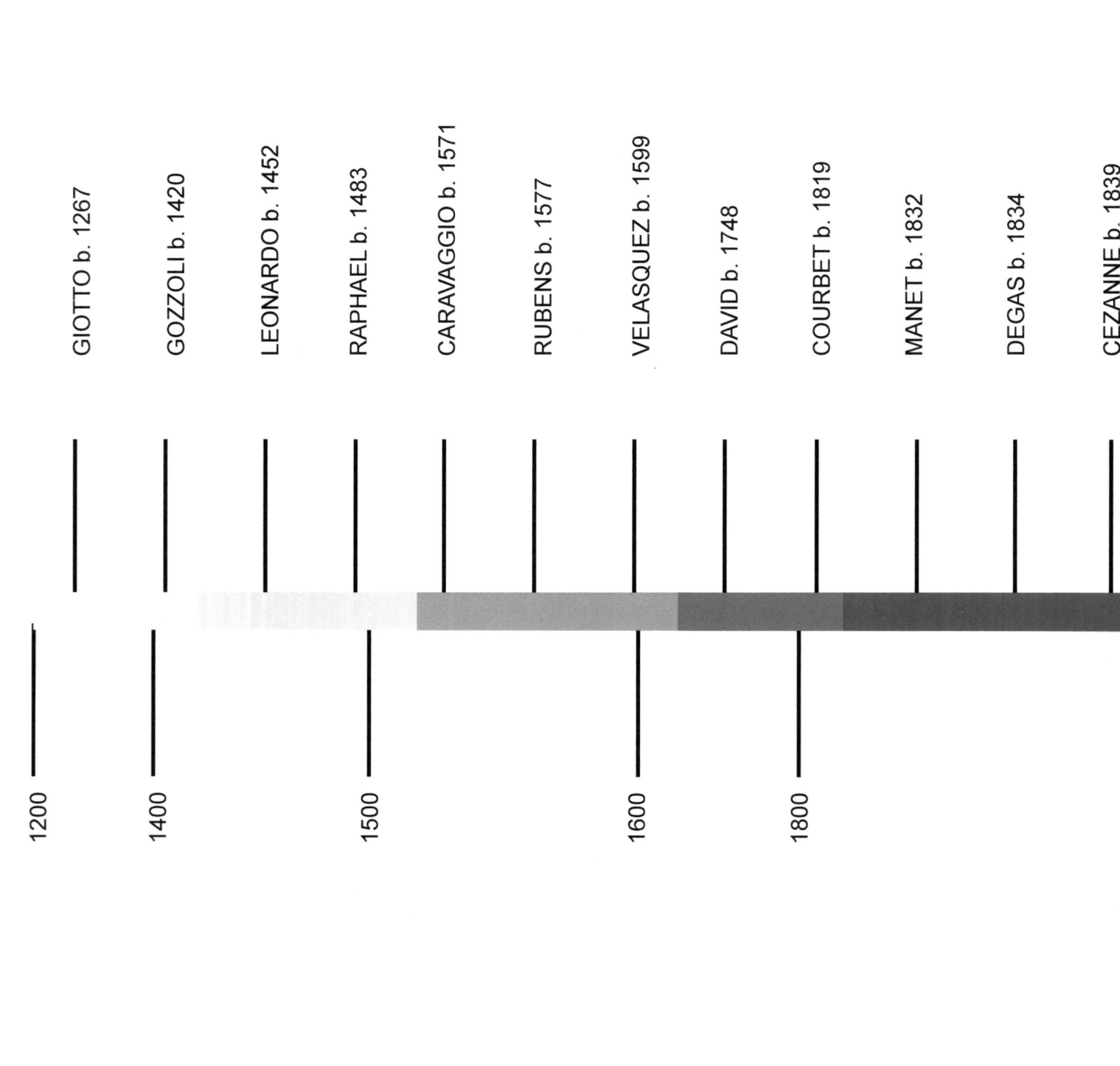

GIOTTO b. 1267

GOZZOLI b. 1420

LEONARDO b. 1452

RAPHAEL b. 1483

CARAVAGGIO b. 1571

RUBENS b. 1577

VELASQUEZ b. 1599

DAVID b. 1748

COURBET b. 1819

MANET b. 1832

DEGAS b. 1834

CEZANNE b. 1839

1200

1400

1500

1600

1800

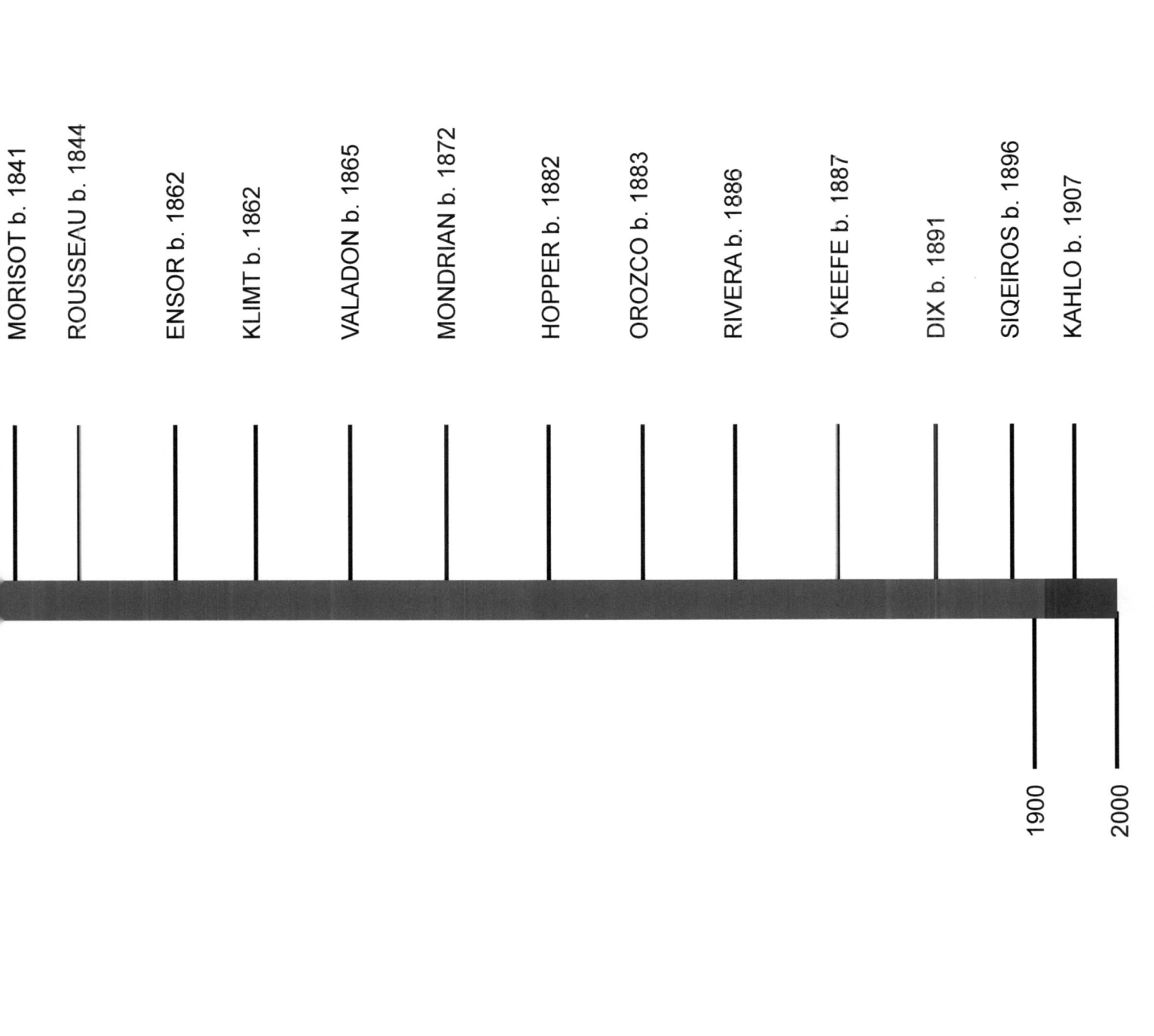

For our grandchildren,

Mahlon, Carlo, Elodie and Wescott

Love,

Crawdad

INTRODUCTION

As I said in my first self-portraits book, copying master self-portraits gives the young or amateurish painter the illusion of knowing and painting like the masters themselves. It doesn't matter if the result in each case is superficial and plagiaristic. It gets the copier closer to the subjects copied and is delightfully pleasant exercise. It may even improve the copier's technical ability.

In a general sense, merely looking at master painters' self-portraits is like meeting the masters. If the viewer is also copying the works it is like painting along side the master in master's own studio or workplace.

The first two self-portraits in this book are of Giotto and Benozzo Gozzoli, both born in Florence, Italy, respectively in 1267 and 1420. At that time and place there was no such thing as a studio self-portrait. Most wall paintings were al fresco, done in churches or palaces and mostly of Biblical subjects. Artists such as Giotto and Gozzoli painted themselves, if at all, in a crowd or procession. Later, as secular subjects dominated European art, Durer, Holbein and Rembrandt, among others, created or nourished a practice of self-portraiture that exists and continues to evolve today.

Leonardo never painted a self-portrait, but his red charcoal drawing is includec in this collection in homage to the greatest painter ever. Self-portraits reveal much about the artist. Caravaggio, for example, led a rough, violent life and he portrayed himself as the served head of Goliath. Raphael reveals in his modest self-portrait his renowned sweetness. Courbet, a bold, dramatic character, portrays himself in a greatly agitated state. Henri Rousseau, perhaps the greatest self-taught, naïve artist, portrays himself in a grand, dignified manner. Klimt, who painted the most beautiful or brilliantly adorned women, never painted his own portrait, saying, "I am less interested as a subject for a painting than I am in other people, above all women." So, Klimt is represented in his collection not by a self-portrait but by a portrait of him by Swiss painter, Ferdinand Hodler. Frida Kahlo painted a great many self-portraits in a wide variety of settings and poses suggesting, perhaps, the turmoil in her own life.

-*Thomas Crawford*

GIOTTO DI BONDONEI

b. 1267, Colle Vespignano (near Florence)

d. 1337, Florence, Italy.

(detail) self-portrait from The Last Judgement panel,

Scrovegni Chapel, Padua.

If Giotto is not the greatest painter, as many believe, he is close to it. His contemporary, Boccacio, who recognized the artists's unequalled brilliance in raising Italian painting from "the grave" of the Middle Ages and onto the threshold of the Renaissance, described Giotto as physically and facially loathesome. In his only self-portrait known to exist, Giotto painted himself as conventionally handsome.

Giotto's masterpieces include: frescoes in the Church of St. Francis, Assisi; all the murals and ceiling in Scrovegni Chapel, Padua; St Francis receiving the stigmata, S. Croce, Florence; and Ognissanti Madonna, Uffizi Gallery, Florence.

BENONZO DI LESE GOZZOLI

1420, Florence, Italy. D. 1497, Pisa.

Self-portrait in fresco, Procession of

The Magi, 1959.

Gozzoli was the chief assistant to Fra Angelico in painting the chapel of Nicolas V in the Vatican. His work on Fra Angelico's St. Lawrence distributing the Treasures of the Church established Gozzoli's reputation as a major, fashionable decorative painter and led to a commission from Piero de Medici to paint a continuous fresco around the walls of the chapel in the Palazzo Medici in Florence. The completed project is the magnificent fresco Procession of the Magi, completed in 1459. Gozzoli painted his own self-portrait as one of the participants in the procession.

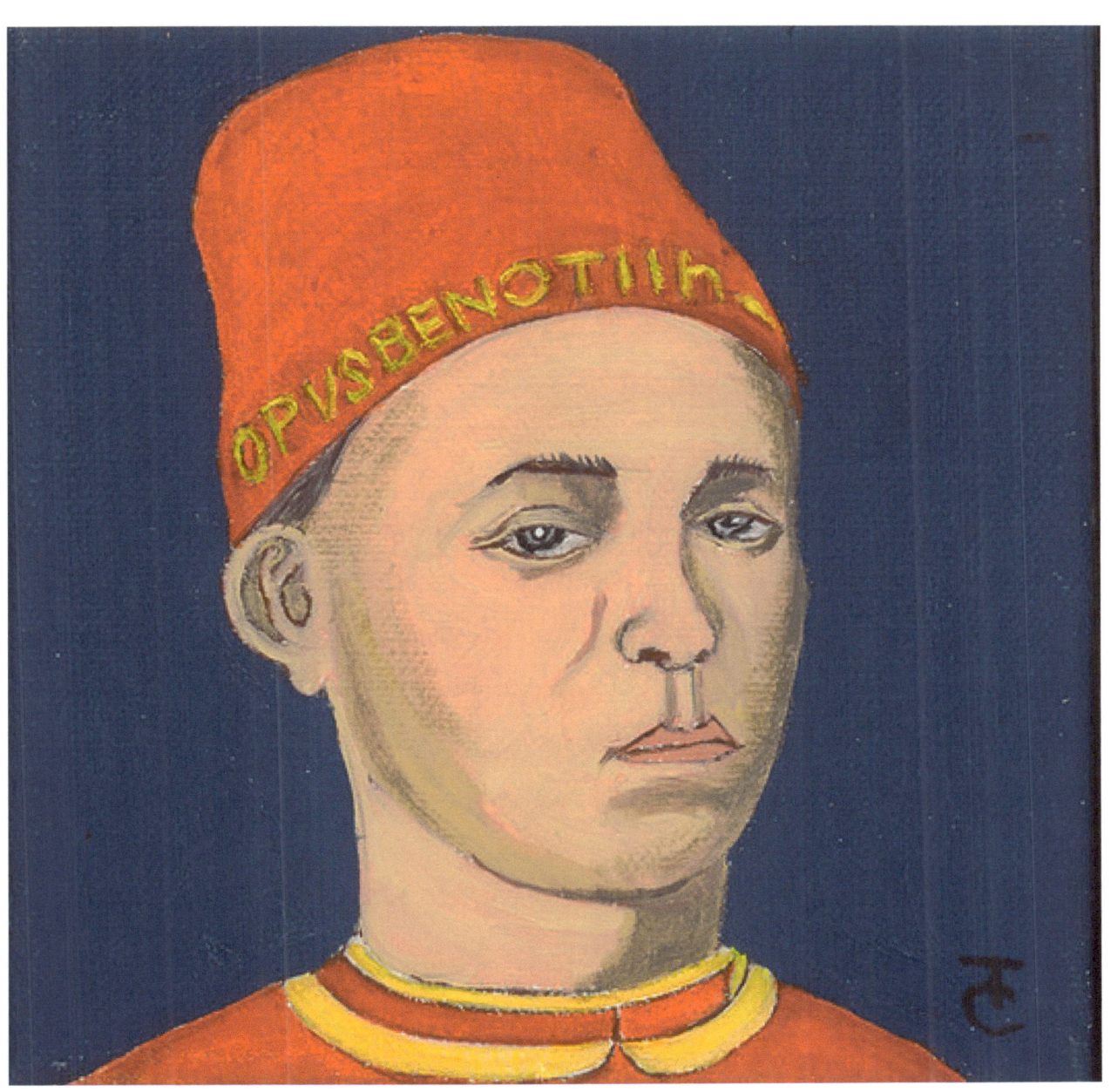

LEONARDO DA VINCI

1452, Vinci, Italy. D. 1519,

Amboise, France.

Self-portrait, red drawing, Turin.

The only surviving self-portrait of the person considered by many to be the greatest artist ever is a red chalk drawing preserved in the Galleria Sabauda, Turin. The creator of the High Renaissance in Florence was not only a great painter but he was ahead of his time in sculpture, architecture, engineering, military science, botany, anatomy, geology, hydraulics, aerodynamics and optics. Leonardo spent his last years and died at a home in Amboise awarded to him by the French king, Francis I. Notable masterpieces are La Gioconda (Mona Lisa) Louvre, Paris; Last Supper. Santa Maria delle Grazie, Milan; Virgin of the Rocks, Louvre; Lady with an Ermine, Czartoryski Collection, Cracow; The Annunciation, Uffizi Gallery, Florence; Madonna of the Rocks, National Gallery, London; Madonna and St. Anne, Louvre; La Belle Ferronniere, Louvre; Portrait of a Musician, Ambrosiana, Milan.

RAFFAELLO SANTI

(known as RAPHAEL)

1483, Urbino. D. 1523, Rome.

Self-portrait from The School of Athens, 1510.

Raphael was born in Urbino, a flourishing center of art and culture, and was introduced at an early age to Perugino, with whom he studied. At age 21 he moved to Florence to be in contact with and under the influence of Leonardo and Michelangelo. His reported natural sweetness of disposition is reflected in this self-portrait from his masterpiece The School of Athens (in the Stanza Della Segnatura, Vatican Palace, Rome) in which the figure of Plato is said to be a portrait of Leonardo. Notable masterpieces include The Mass of Bolsena, Stanza di Eliodoro, Vatican Palace; St. George and the Dragon, Louvre; Vision of a Knight, National Gallery, London; Portrait of Angelo Doni, Pitti Palace, Florence; Portrait of a Cardinal, Prado, Madrid; Madonna of the Goldfinch, Uffizi, Florence.

MICHAELANGELO MERISI, called CARAVAGGIO

1571, Caravaggio, Duchy of Milan.

d. 1610, Porto Ercole, Grand Duchy of Tuscany.

Self-portrait as the head of Goliath in David with the head

of Goliath, 1605, Galleria Borghese, Rome.

It is not surprising that Caravaggio's self-portrait is shocking. His short life of 38 years was a mix of brilliant, innovative painting and violent, even criminal homicidal behavior. His use of chiaroscuro (the technique of shifting from light to dark with little intermediate value) was unsurpassed and had a singularly profound effect on Baroque painting.

His masterpieces include: The Calling of Saint Matthew, Contarelli Chapel, San Luigi dei Frances', Rome; The Crucifixion of Saint Peter, Cerasi Chapel, Santa Maria del Popolo, Rome; The Fortune Teller, Accademia Carrara, Bergamo; The Conversion of St. Paul, Church of Santa Maria Del Popolo, Rome; Adoration of the Shepherds, Museo Nazionale, Messina; Bacchus Ailing, Borghese Gallery, Rome.

PETER PAUL RUBENS

1577, Siegenn, Nassau-Dillenburg, Holy Roman Empire.

d. 1640, Antwerp, Belgium.

Self-portrait in The Honeysuckle Bower, 1609,

Alte Pinakothek Museum, Vienna.

Rubens, the premier Flemish Baroque artist, was one of the most prolific painters ever and one of the most prosperous because of his appeal to Europe's nobility and to the wealthiest art collectors of his time. The portrait of Rubens and his first wife The Honeysuckle Bower shows the elegance and extravagance typical of his life and work.

Other notable paintings are: Descent from the Cross, Hermitage, St. Petersburg; Rape of the Daughters of Leucippus, Alte Pinakothek; The Fall of Man, Prado; The Feast of Venus and Portrait of Helene Fourment, both in Kunsthistoriches Museum, Vienna; The Fall of Phaeton, National Gallery of Art, Washington, D.C.

DIEGO VELASQUEZ

1599, Seville, Spain. D. 1660, Madrid.

self-portrait from The Maids of Honor

("Las Meninas") 1665, Prado.

Velasquez, born in Seville of Portuguese immigrants, painted most of his life in the service of Spanish King Philip IV. His self-portrait in his masterpiece, Las Meninas, reflects his attachment to courtesan society, his reserved, undramatic approach to art, and his faultless technique in the logic of light and shade. It is said that Manet's style of impressionism was influenced by Velasquez and that both Picasso and Dali paid repeated tribute to the Spanish master by recreating his most famous works.

Notable paintings include: The Surrender of Breda, Prado, Madrid; Innocent X, Doria Pamphili Gallery, Rome; El Triunfo de Baco, Prado; Portrait of Juan de Pareja, Metropolitan Museum of Art, New York.

JACQUES-LOUIS DAVID

1748, Paris. D. 1825, Brussels.

Self-portrait, 1794, Louvre.

David's self-portrait painted in 1794 must be the only self-portrait painted by a master in prison. David, founder of the French classical school, was, perhaps, the most political of all painters. He supported the French Revolution, was connected to Robespierre, sketched Maria Antoinette on her way to the guillotine and as a member of the Committee of Public Safety voted for the death of Napoleon XVI. After 1804 he was the painter in Napoleon's court and was later exiled to Brussels. His master pieces include: The Death of Marat, Royal Museum of Fine Arts, Brussels; The Death of Socrates, and Mlle. Charlotte Du Val D'Ognes, Metropolitan Museum of Art, New York; Sappho and Phaon, Hermitage, St. Petersburg; Comtesse Daru, Frick Collection, New York; Napoleon in his Study, and The Battle of the Romans and Sabines, Louvre, Paris.

GUSTAVE COURBET

1819, Ornans, France. D. 1877,

La Tour-de-Peliz, Switzerland

Self-portrait "The Desperate Man," c. 1844, private collection,

Courbet initiated the movement against painters like David and Ingres, who painted historical and classical subjects, by concentrating on realistic paintings of common subjects. Known for his fiercely independent spirit in art and life, Courbet was associated with the communists in the Revolution of 1871 that led to his imprisonment and eventual exile. Among his master pieces are: A Burial at Ornans, Artist's Studio, Cliffs at Etretat, The Origin of the World, Nude Woman with a Dog, all at Musee d'Orsay; Roe-Deer in the Forest, Louvre; and The Beautiful Irishwoman, Metropolitan Museum of Art, New York.

EDOUARD MANET

1832, Paris. D. 1833, Paris

self-portrait, 1878, Loed Collection, New York.

A pivotal figure in the transition from realism to impressionism, Manet was probably the most important 19th century artist to paint contemporary life. Two of his paintings completed in 1893, Le Dejeuner Sur L'Herbe (Louvre) and Olympia (Musee d'Orsay) were highly controversial when first exhibited but inspired young painters and mark the genesis of modern art. Manet was a bridge between Corot and Courbet, on one hand, and the impressionists, on the other, and was a friend to all. Although Manet was a great portrait artist he did only two indifferent self-portraits, including this one.

Other masterpieces: The Bar of the Follies-Bergeres, Courtauld Gallery, London; Boating, Metropolitan Museum of Art, New York; The Railway, National Gallery of Art, Washington, D.C.; and many works at the Musee d'Orsay, Paris, including The Balcony, Berthe Morisot with a Bouquet of Violets, Portrait of Emile Zola, Portrait of Stephen Mallarme, and Young Flautist.

EDGAR DEGAS

1834, Paris. D. 1917 Paris.

self-portrait, 1895, Arp Museum Bahnhof Rolandser.

Degas was one of the founders of Impressionism but he rejected the term preferring to be called a realist, and though he exhibited with his fellow impressionists, he maintained a separateness from them in life and art. Renoir reportedly deplored Degas' argumentative nature and said, "All his (Degas') friends had to leave him," and Renoir was the last to go. Degas was a superb draftsman whose extraordinary talent is evident in paintings, sculptures, prints and drawings. He was a master of depicting movement in paintings of dancers, racecourses and female nudes. Among his masterpieces are: L'Absinthe, Le Tub, Rose-Adelaide De Gas, Etude de Mains, and Jockeys Devant les Tribunes, all at the Louvre, Paris; La Femme Aux Chtysanthemenes and Le Foyer de La Danse, both at the Metropolitan Museum, New York; Aux Bains de Mer, National Gallery, London; and Pendant La Lecon De Danse, Museum of Art, Philadelphia.

PAUL CEZANNE

1839, Aix-en-Province, France.

d. 1906, Aix-en-Province.

Self-portrait, 1876, Neue Staatsgalerie, Munich.

Though recognized by Picasso and Matisse as the father of modern art, Cezanne was curiously alienated from his Impressionist friends and estranged from the modern art public who admired his work. Renoir reportedly praised Cezanne, saying that he could not place two colors side by side without producing remarkable effects. He worked largely in isolation, painting subjects and objects nearby and landscapes outside his home in southern France. He was not a particularly good portrait artist but painted 42 self-portraits. Some of his masterpieces are: L'Estaque, Metropolitan Museum of Art, New York; Card Players, Stephen C. Clark Collection, New York; Bathers and Still Life with Apples, both in the Museum of Modern Art, New York; Mont Sainte Victoire, Courtauld Institute of Art, London; Jas de Bouffan, Minneapolis Institute of Art; The Basket of Apples, Art Institute of Chicago; The Bathers, National Gallery, London; Big Pine near Aix, Hermitage, St. Petersburg.

BERTHE MORISOT

1841,Bourges, Cher, France.

d. 1895, Paris.

self-portrait, 1885, Musee Marmattan Monet, Paris.

Morisot was a major figure in the premier group of seven French Impressionists who spurned the Academicians' Salon and had the first of their own exhibitions in 1874. One contemporary art critic said of her, "no one represents Impressionism with more refined talent or more authority than Morisot.", Her superb plein air landscapes are complemented by beautiful impressionist interior compositions. An excellent portraitist herself, she was also the subject of or model in several celebrated paintings by her brother-in-law, Edouard Manet. Notable masterpieces include: Grain field and The Cradle, both in Musee D'Orsay; La Coiffure, Museo Nacional de Buenos Aires; Fillette lisant, Museum of Fine Arts, St. Petersburg; L'lle du Bois de Boulogne, National Gallery of Art, Washington, D.C.; Mme. Boursier and her Daughter, Brooklyn Museum; The Artist's Daughter Julie with her Nanny, Minneapolis Institute of Art.

HENRI ROUSSEAU

1844, Laval, Mayenne, France. D. 1910, Paris.

Self-portrait, 1890, Narodni Gallery, Prague.

Rousseau is almost universally acclaimed to be the greatest self-taught or naive artist ever. He started painting seriously in his early forties and at age 49 retired from his job as a toll collector and painted full-time. He was known as Le Douanier (the customs officer) and was routinely ridiculed during his lifetime by critics. In spite of this, he produced a dozen magnificent canvases, including one of the most penetrating indictments of war, entitled War,1894, the Louvre, Paris. Other masterpieces include Head of Monkey, Collection Georges Renand, Paris; Flowers in Vase, Albright Art Gallery, Buffalo; Jadwiga's Dream, Museum of Modern Art, New York; Ballplayers, Collection Mrs. Henry D. Sharpe, Providence, RI.; Country Wedding, Private Collection, Paris; Sleeping Gypsy, Museum of Modern Art, New York; Pierre Loti, Kunthaus, Zurich. and Exotic Landscape, Private Collection, Zurich.

JAMES ENSOR

1860, Ostend, Belgium. d. 1949, Ostend.

Self-portrait with Masks, 1899,

Cleomir Juissiant Collecion, Antwerp.

After attending art school in Brussels, Ensor worked for 17 years in his studio in his parents' attic. He traveled little outside Brussels. He admired Rubens and Bosch and alluded to their works in several of his own paintings. He favored tumultuous compositions of brilliant color, often depicting masks or situations of self-mockery. He painted his master piece, Entry of Christ into Brussels at age 29 and Self-portrait with Masks at 39. Thereafter, until his death 50 years later, he painted not a single work that added to his reputation, according to several critics. Although he stood apart from other artists, he significantly influenced Paul Klee, Emile Nolde , George Grosz and other expressionist and surrealist artists of his time. Distinguished works include: Entry of Christ into Brussels, J. Paul Getty Museum, Los Angeles; The Rower, Koninklijk Museum voor Schone, Kubsten, Antwerp; Intrigue, Royal Museum of Fine Arts, Antwerp.

GUSTAVE KLIMT

b. 1862, Vienna, Austria. d. 1918, Vienna.

Portrait of Klimt painted by Ferdinand Hodler in 1916.

Early in his career, Klimt was a successful painter of conventionally rendered architectural decorations. As he developed a more personal style, he concentrated on the female body as his primary subject, done in a frankly erotic manner. He used gold leaf in his erotic paintings, creating brilliant, beautiful works, which were much prized and sought after. Klimt greatly influenced his Austrian contemporary, Egon Schiele.

The portrait above is not Klimt's self-portrait but rather a portrait by Ferdinand Hodler. It is included in this collection because like self-portraits it reveals much about the subject and is a delightful addition. This is what Klimt said about self-portraits:

"I have never painted a sell-portrait. I am less interested in myself as a subject for a painting than I am in other people, above all women... There is nothing special about me. I am a painter who paints day after day from morning to night...Who ever wants to know something about me...ought to look carefully at my pictures."

Notable works include: The Kiss, and Judith I (und du Kopf des Holofernes) both in Osterreich Galerie Belvedere, Vienna; Judith II (Salome), Ca Pesaro Galleria Internazionale d'Arte Moderna, Musei Civica, Venice; Die Hoffnung II, Metropolitan Museum of Art, New York; Portrait of Margaret Stoneborough-Wittgenstein, Neue Pinakothek, Munich; Portrait of Adele Block-Bauer II, Private Collection; Horticultural Landscape with Hilltop, Kunsthaus Zug, Stiftung Sammburg Kamm.

SUZANNE VALADON

1865, Bessines, France. D. 1938, Paris.

Self-portrait in a group, 1912, Pomaret Collection,

Nice, Aix-en-Provence.

Unlike her affluent and privileged contempories, Morisot and Cassatt, Valadon was the daughter of an unmarried laundress. At a young age she and her mother moved from a provincial town to Montmartre, Paris, where Valadon eventually performed in a circus. In her teens, she suffered a bad fall from a trapeze and consequently took to earning her living as an artist's model. She modeled for several paintings by Morisot, Renoir, Chavannes and Toulouse-Lautrec and was encouraged in her own painting pursuits by Degas. Her association with prominent painters accelerated the critical and popular acceptance her work received. She tutored her son, Maurice Utrillo, who became a celebrated painter as prominently celebrated as his mother. Significant paintings by Valadon include the following: Eric Satie, Centre Georges Pompidou, Paris, France; Self-portrait, Georges Pompidou Center, Paris, France; After the bath, Petit Palais, Geneva; Adam and Eve, Georges Pompidou Center, Paris, France; Casting the Net, Georges Pompidou Center, Paris, France; Roses in a Vase, Private Collection; Portrait of a Woman, Wallraf-Richartz Museum, Cologne, Germany.

PIET MONDRIAN

1872, Amsfoort, Netherlands. D. 1944, New York.

self-portrait, 1918, The Hague.

Widely considered a leading figure of early abstract painting, Mondrian was (and is today) the strictest and most "architectural" of all abstract painters. As he moved from Amsterdam to Paris and then to New York, his work evolved from impressionistic pastoral images to a tentative abstract style influenced by Cubism and finally to a style in which his pictures are composed entirely of solid squares or rectangles with all lines going either perfectly vertical or horizontal. Some notable works are: Spring Sun (Lentzon) Castle Ruin, Dallas Museum of Art; Flowering Trees, Nieuwenhuizen Segaar Art Gallery, The Hague; Broadway Boogie-Woogie, Museum of Modern Art, New York; Composition No. 10, The Hague; Composition with Red, Yellow and Blue, The Kroeller-Muller Museum, Otterlo, Netherlands; Composition in White and Blue, Philadelphia Museum of Art.

EDWARD HOPPER

1882, upper Nyack, New York. D. 1967, New York City.

self-portrait, 1925-30, Whitney Museum of American Art,

New York.

Hopper, a realist painter never tempted by abstract art or the styles of other modern artists, probably created a body of work whose imagery has imprinted itself more powerfully on the way America views itself than any other artist. His modern American landscapes show us small towns, suburbs, icons of our automobile culture, and familiar urban spaces of diners and theaters. Hopper was a slow, methodical painter who eschewed flashy brush strokes and flourishes in favor of careful renderings with just the right mix of light and shade to create the mood he wanted. Notable works include: Night Hawks, Art Institute of Chicago; Automat, Des Moines Art Center, Iowa; Chop Suey, Barney Ebsworth Collection, St. Louis Art Museum; Early Sunday Morning, Railroad Sunset, and Second Story Sunlight, all in Whitney Museum of American Art, New York; Office at Night, Walker Art Center, Minneapolis; Hotel Lobby, Indianapolis Museum of Art; Office in a Small City, Metropolitan Museum of Art, New York; Cape Cod Evening, National Gallery of Art, Washington, D.C.; Lighthouse Hill, Dallas Museum of Art; New York Movie, Museum of Modern Art, New York; Summertime, Delaware Art Museum, Wilmington.

JOSE CLEMENTE OROZCO

1883, Ciudad Guzman Mexico. d. 1949, Mexico City.

self-portrait, location unknown.

Orozco, along with Rivera and Siqueiros, was the leading practitioner of the Mexico Mural Renaissance. The most politically committed of the three, Orozco promoted the political causes of peasants and workers. From 1922 to 1926 he painted heroic murals in Mexico City. From 1927 to 1934 he lived in the U.S.A., during which time he painted the Prometheus mural at Pomona College and his magnificent series of murals in the library of Dartmouth College. He returned to Mexico in 1935 and painted additional murals in Mexico City and Guadalajara. Notable works include: The Epic of American Civilization, Dartmouth College, New Hampshire; Prometheus, Pomona College, California; painting of Miguel Hidalgo y Castilla, Jalisco Governmental Palace, Guadalajara; Omnisciencia, House of Tiles, Mexico City; The People and Its Leaders, Government Palace, Guadalajara; Christ Destroying His Cross, Museo de Arte Alvar y Carmen T. de Carrillo Gil. Mexico.

DIEGO RIVERA

1886, Guanajuato, Mexico. d. 1957, Mexico City.

self-portrait, 1954, Detroit Institute of Art.

Rivera, the best known of the "Big Three" of the Mexican Mural Renaissance, was influenced, early in his career by Cubism, then shifted to a Cezannesque Post-Impressionisrn style before becoming involved in a government sponsored mural program. He developed his own style based on large, simplified figures and bold colors that depicted Mexican society and reflected Mexico's 1910 Revolution. Rivera was an atheist and a communist; a friend of Amadeo Modigliani and Leon Trotsky; and was twice married to Frida Kahlo. Notable works include: Creation, Bolivar Auditorium, National Preparatory School, Mexico City; Man, Controller of the Universe, Palacio de Bellas Artes, Mexico City; Tierra Fecunda, Chapingo Autonomous University of Agriculture, Mexico City; Man and Machinery, Institute of Arts, Detroit; Day of the Dead, In the Trenches, and Orgy - Night of the Rich, all in the Ministry of Education, Mexico City; The Huastec Civilization, Palacio Nacional, Mexico City.

GEORGIA O'KEEFFE

1887, Sun Prairie, Wisconsin. D. 1986,

Santa Fe, New Mexico.

Self-portrait, private collection.

O'Keeffe, best known for her paintings of enlarged flowers, New York skyscrapers and New Mexico landscapes, also, is celebrated for the sensual and feminist imagery in her paintings. She was married to renowned photographer, Alfred Stieglitz, who often photographed her during their life together in New York. After his death, O'Keeffe moved to New Mexico, where for the rest of her long life she created unforgettable images of that part of America. Notable works include: Cow's Skull, Red, White and Blue, Metropolitan Museum of Art, New York; Ram's Head White Hollyhock and Little Hills, The Brooklyn Museum, New York; Blue and Green Music, Art Institute of Chicago, Illinois; Jimson Weed, Indianapolis Museum of Art; Abstraction White Rose and Calla Lily in Tall Glass, both at Georgia O'Keeffe Museum, Santa Fe, New Mexico, Black Iris VI, Curtis Galleries, Minneapolis.

OTTO DIX

1891, Untermhaus, Gera, Germany. d. 1969, Singen,

Baden-Wurttemberg, Germany.

Self-portrait, 1913, Detroit Institute of Art, Michigan.

Dix was an art student in Dresden when World War I broke out. He volunteered for the German Army, fought on both the Eastern and Western fronts, was wounded and earned the Iron Cross. Between wars he lived and painted in Dresden and Berlin, and traveled to Paris, Vienna and Switzerland. He is best known for his ruthlessly realistic depictions of Weimar society and the brutality of war and the Nazis confiscated and destroyed at least three paintings considered to be degenerate. More than 1,500 of his works were hidden away and saved by an art dealer and found by his son in 2012. Among his masterpieces are: Trenches, private collection; Shell Craters, Leipzig Museum of Fine Arts; Farewell to Hamburg, Galerie Gunzenhauser, Munich; To Beauty, Von der Heydt Museum, Wurppertal; The Match Vendor, Staatsgalerie, Stuttgart; Portrait of the Journalist Slyvia von Harden, Musee National d'Arte Moderne, Paris; Portrait of the Dancer Anita Berber and Boig City (Triptych) both in Stuttgart Municipal Gallery.

DAVID ALFARO SIQUEIROS

1896, Camargo, Chihuahua.

d. 1974, Cuernavaca, morelos, Mexico.

self-portrait, 1945, Museo Nacional del Arte, Mexico City.

Sequeiros, one of the "Big Three" Mexican muralists, was said by Rivera "to think of himself as very handsome and very terrible." He was a member of the Mexican Communist Party who participated in an unsuccessful attempt to assassinate Leon Trotsky in 1940. Always deeply active in politics, he believed that his art and politics were intricately intertwined. In addition to his primary base in Mexico City, Siqueiros worked in New York City Notable works are: Ethnography, The Museum of Modern Art, New York, Don Porfirio and his Courtesans, Revolutionary on a Horse and The People in Arms, all three murals at Museo Nacional de Historica, Mexico City; Burial of a Worker, Colegio Chico, Mexico City; mural in Hospital de la Raza, Mexico City; paintings Feminine Torso and Three Calabashes in Museo de Arte Alvar y Carmen T. de Carillo Gil, Mexico City; The March of Humanity, Polyforum Cultural Siqueiros, Mexico City.

FRIDA KAHLO

1907, Coyocan, Mexico. d. 1954, Coyocan.

Self-portrait dedicated to Sigmund Firestone, 1940,

Private collection.

Kahlo contracted polio as a child and suffered serious injuries in her teens as a result of a traffic accident. Of at least 140 paintings she created 55 are self-portraits. She is reported to have said, "I paint myself because I am so often alone and because I am the subject I know best." Suggestions of pain are present in many of her works owing to her illnesses, injuries, several miscarriages and a very troubled marriage to her mentor, painter Diego Rivera. Among her most notable paintings are: The Frame, Centre Pompidou, Paris; Self-portrait with Cropped Hair, Museum of Modern Art, New York; Diego on my Mind, The Jacques and Natasha Gelman Collection of Modern and Contemporary Art; Fruits of the Earth, Collection Banco Nacional de Mexico, Mexico City; Self-Portrait with Monkey, Albright-Knox Gallery, Buffalo; Self-portrait on the Borderline Between Mexico and the United States, Collection of Maria Rodriguez de Reyero.